Table

Preface

Why This Book Was Written

Teish's Voice:

I am walking through the sands of Egypt, where ancient sculptures hold thousands of years of history and the remains of a great civilization. I am awe struck to be able to walk this path, to breathe this air, and to witness the magnificence of our human history. As my feet push against the hot desert sand, my eyes behold a sight they cannot believe. I see a burning ember being pushed into the stone of this great edifice, the great Pyramids at Giza. My eyes follow the fire and meet the sight of a pale hand, hairy and sweaty that leads along an arm covered with sandy blond hair. I am shocked, stunned and numbed to realize that a member of my party, a Euro-American man, has just put his cigarette out on the walls of the great pyramids!

Another time and place brings another example, of people's disregard for the sacred. I am leading a group of women on a sacred site tour in the mountains of Jamaica. We crawl down into a cave and swing like ancient women on the roots of great trees and land in the belly of a white coral cave. Before I can say or do anything to begin the ritual, which would honor the fact that we have been allowed to enter this sacred place, I gasp in horror as I see one of the women reach down and pick up a human bone. Doesn't she know that this is an ancient Arawak burial ground? Doesn't she know that it is sacrilege to grab any sacred object without permission? She doesn't know! And I don't know why she does not know.

Behaviors such as these are painfully disrespectful. I have spent 30 years of my life responding to incidences and attitudes such as this. And I succumbed to both anger and depression by refusing to conduct any more sacred site tours. This made for a great contradiction because I love to travel in groups and regard everywhere on Earth as sacred while recognizing that certain places hold particularly powerful energy. So many people have asked me to resume my sacred site tours but I cannot bear to be a part of the gross ignorance and disrespect that characterizes the tourist mentality. Walking that path has been both a frustrating and enlightening experience for me.

i

This book is designed to reconcile the contradiction. It is my hope that the material presented here will educate the well-intended person and we can go forward together to praise the sacredness of Mother Earth. And it is the primary reason why I am writing this book.

Leilani's Voice:

It is the month of August in the year 2000. More than 1000 people from all over the world have gathered at a conference on the Big Island of Hawai'i to celebrate the Sacred Hula.

The Big Island of Hawai'i is a place where many of the ancient customs and traditions of our Hawaiian ancestors have been preserved. It is the home of Tutu Pele, Goddess of Fire, the volcano, Our Grandmother and sacred elder. It is the place where new Earth is created daily as lava meets ocean, steam rises from the sea to the clouds and balls of fire float in the water. All the elements are in their full glory along with the beauty of the warm tropical rain showers and banyan trees that are as large as three story buildings.

The kumu, the head teacher/elder informs the people of the proper protocols for participating in this gathering. We are told that the elders have granted permission for us to be here and for certain chants and songs to be used only on this occasion. It is explained to us that this is an event that requires collective effort and concentration. We are especially asked not to wander off into individual meditations, movements or other distractions. And most importantly, we are told not to trample the land, not touch sacred objects, not to disturb the altars, and not to take photographs. It was made clear that this was a sacred gathering rather than a tourist attraction.

We broke up into focus groups of about 50 people each and my group accepted the assignment to plant young Hala and Coconut trees on Hawaiian Homestead land. This land is regarded as particularly important because it has been reclaimed by the Native Hawaiian people and is looked upon as sacred. So, we are singing as we plant. The song asks that fertility and prosperity return to the land. It is important to focus on awakening this energy.

However, at a heightened point in the ritual my concentration and connection is disturbed by an intruder who approached me from behind. I turned around to find a Mainland Haole (Euro-American) woman handing me her camera and insisting that I take a photograph of her. She was not in the process of planting.

Briefly, I explained to her that her concentration should have been on the sacredness of the land, not on having her picture taken. It was a moment for reverence not vanity. I couldn't really take the time to educate her on the importance of sacred site etiquette because I was in ritual protocol. I did not see this woman for the rest of the conference and was left wondering if she fully understood her actions.

This is just one of many experiences that reinforce my belief that many people simply do not realize how sacred the Earth is and the impact of their behavior upon it. Educating people on these matters is my main motivation for writing this book.

The decision to write this book is born out of 20-30 years of experience.

We are blessed to be two women of color who have grown up in a spiritual culture that has survived centuries of oppression and kept its regard for the sacredness of land in tact and in the forefront of our behavior and rituals.

However, we also recognize that ritual protocol is not taught in school and is not available even in schools with Spirituality Departments and in only a few of the books presently on the shelf.

We long for the reconstruction of a culture that respects the Earth and Her people. Our present ecological crisis: global warming, water and air pollution, starvation and war are all manifestations of our disregard for the Earth, Her gifts and Her children.

The world needs leadership that emphasizes Reverence, Community, and Peacekeeping. And this can only happen in an atmosphere of mutual respect and sharing. We must do this without arrogance and we must overcome our ignorance.

We decided to write this book as an offering of guidelines and protocols to heal our relationship to sacred lands and to each other. We encourage its use as a means to insure the re-creation of our Earth-centered traditions and the evolution of a global and authentic spiritual practice.

How This Book Is Written

This is a collaborative effort.

We are sharing both the power and the responsibility for the content of this book and the voices in which it is written. We have chosen to speak in a language that is personal, communal, instructive, and accessible. The names of deities and their personal pronouns are capitalized as a demonstration of respect for our own traditions. To reserve capitalization only for the word God implies subscription to the Judeo/Christian male deity as the Ultimate Power. This is not our belief.

The book is filled with our personal stories and the adventures we have experienced in our travels as teachers and priestesses. Wherever possible the stories have been told exactly as they occurred. Some stories **may be** written in the style of myth in order to illustrate the Universal Truth of the experience while protecting the identity of the individuals.

This book is composed of three Chapters: **Walking the Land, The Earth Is Our Mother**, and **Passageways.**

In the first chapter entitled **"Walking the Land,"** we share our personal stories, myths, and histories. This chapter also contains an exercise, which will help you to get in touch with your personal experience and relationship to Holy Ground.

The second chapter is entitled **"The Earth Is Our Mother"**. This chapter contains a section which provides instructions, guidelines, and recommendations drawn from the protocols of our respective cultures, which can and will inform you of their essence and importance. This will help you to understand their purpose and function so that you can participate respectfully in sacred site tours.

We also provide you with instructions, examples and advice for creating rituals to honor Earth, Air, Fire, and Water as the body of the Living Goddess. We are sure you will find this material helpful.

The third chapter, "**Passageways**" offers a sampling of protocols for traversing sacred space with cultural sensitivity. They include examples of proper greetings and salutations, definitions of sacred boundaries, attaining permission to participate in rituals and other ways to express your sacred intentions. This chapter also includes a series of questions, which will help you to avoid the "tourist traps" so prevalent in modern travel.

The book culminates with an Oath to Mother Earth. The reader is asked to sign their name to this pledge as a commitment to devotional passages on Holy Ground.

We recommend that you read this book from cover to cover first. Savor the stories and allow their meaning to become a natural part of your understanding. Return to this work as a reference and put the guidelines to practice. Then contact us for lectures, workshops, and when you need support to go forward into the world.

May you walk good upon our beautiful Earth.

Ashe-Aloha

Leilani and Teish

"I have stood silently in awe of the rainforest in Africa, the South Pacific and the Caribbean. I have walked down dusty roads in Mexico and said prayers to the pyramid of the moon. I have watched the volcano erupt and followed Her lava flow to the sea."   Luisah Teish

Chapter One
Walking the Land

Goddess Haumea, Goddess Papa

In the beginning,
the land was created by the union of Papa, known as Earth Mother
and Father Wakea—Sky God. Through their union,
it is believed that the Hawaiian Islands were born.
Papa, Earth Mother is also known by the name of Haumea,
it is she who birthed the land and the people of the Land. It is she who helps
women in childbirth; thus she is the patroness and Goddess of childbirth.
Papa or Haumea is the mother of all other Hawaiian Goddesses—they are
her daughters.

It is she who is the mother of island chiefesses and ancestresses of our Hawaiian people. Papa/Haumea are both symbolic of the female principal. Her traditional home is the Sacred Nu'umealani, one of the mythical islands of the Akua/Gods.
It is also believed her home is in Kalihi Valley on O'ahu. -
~Leilani Birely~

The Goddess Haumea has many names and appears in many places in Hawai'i. She is our Hawaiian Earth Mother and is responsible for the beauty of the Hawaiian Islands and great respect is given to her. She is the one who helps women in childbirth and the fertility of the land. The breadfruit tree is sacred to her. Myths connected with her name tell of her as a goddess from Nu'umealani. She has the power to change her form and to alter youth to age or from age to youth through the possession of a marvelous fish-drawing branch called Makalei. The stick or Makalei tree is associated as a tree with never ending food supply. In the Hawaiian dictionary, Makalei is defined as: 1. Fish Branch 2. Name of a supernatural tree found on Moloka'i; portions of its root were placed by the gates of fishponds, as they were thought to attract fish.

In legend and chants, Haumea is sometimes associated with La'ila'i who was the first human woman who was born along with the gods Kane and Kanaloa and the man Ki'i. In the Kumulipo, which is considered by many (natives as well as scholars) to be a documentation of Hawaiian genealogy, the woman La'ila'i is named the first human being. It is said that the first human La'ila'i and her ancestors and parents were of the night—he po wale no, that she was the progenitor of the Hawaiian race.

Haumea as listed in the Pukui Elbert Hawaiian dictionary, "known also as Kameha'ikana, the great source of the family and fertility who bore children in successive generations. She is also called Haumea of mysterious forms, Haumea of eightfold forms, Haumea of four-hundred-thousand fold forms..."

Kameha'ikana is the variant name when associated with breadfruit trees. Thus the low-lying bush form, 'Uluhua I Ka Hapapa variety of breadfruit is sacred to her. There is a myth about Haumea as Kameha'ikana in which she transforms into a breadfruit tree in the uplands of Kalihi Valley on O'ahu. Kameha'ikana is one of the names for the wondrous (kameha'i) goddess Haumea, who presided over childbirth. She was thought to have borne

2

numerous children to one husband, then to have gone to Kahiki (another version used interchangeably with Tahiti), later returning as a young woman to bear many more children; she did this for many generations; hence her name is synonymous with prolificness. The statement *he hanauna kameha'ikana lakou*, means they are a generation extremely numerous.

Haumea, as well as being the goddess of childbirth, is also the goddess of fertility and the wild plants of the forest. When we experience the lushness, fertility, and richness of the land of Hawai'i we are in touch with her presence. The elements of nature are represented through Papa-Haumea.

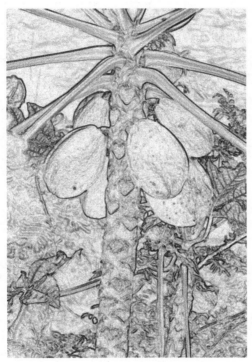

© Picture by Eden Sussenguth

Leilani's Childhood:

Since childhood, my ancestral lineage to the Hawaiian people and the Aina/Land has called to me strongly and it still does. I grew up around Ohana/family where there was a melting pot of languages spoken by the elders. Aunties from Grandpa's side of the family spoke a mixture of Hawaiian, Chinese and pigeon English. As kids, we were lucky to pick up every other sentence or so.

3

As a young girl, I was mesmerized by the storytelling of my Grandma Yolanthe Leimomi Chong, and older cousins, aunts, and uncles about the Hawaiian legends. My sisters and I sat as wide-eyed children listening to legends of Pele and Hawaiian spirits. These precious storytelling times are clear in my memory. I now know that I was being taught about the sacred customs and tabus of our heritage. Most importantly, I was being taught that all things that are powerful must be respected.

From my girlhood, I remember listening-- how no one dared to drive passed the Pali (an area on the island of Oahu) with pork in their car lest they come upon the wrath of Pele. Stories about unfortunate souls who broke the sacred Kapu (taboo) brought terror to my soul; cars were known to drive off the cliff or mysteriously vanish. We also listened about the old woman who was often seen hitch hiking on the road and graciously given a ride only to disappear from the back seat of the car. This was known to be Pele. She sometimes would also change from an old woman to a young maiden. Stories about those that had actually seen the ghost Ali'i (royalty/sacred ones) and warriors haunted my body at bedtime. If you had the bad luck to come upon the Ali'i ghosts one had to strip down naked and prostrate as no one could look upon the Ali'i even in their spirit form.

The tales my Grandma told during our summer vacations in Hawai'i fascinated my three sisters, Paris, Cyd, Tanya and me. She would tell about the akulele, an invisible demon spirit, which could bite you during the night and leave bruises and marks on one's body. I remember lying in bed at night listening to the way the wind would talk at night, through the trees and the way the shadows would dance through the Venetian blinds and cause them to moan and whisper. It was a place of mystery as well as fear.

We were also told stories of those who did not respect the land--of tourists who would come to Hawai'i and disregard the kapu of taking rocks from the islands home with them. It is forbidden to take rocks away from the islands. The rocks are part of the body of the island-- of Papa Haumea. Would you want someone to come up to you, take something from your body, and take it home? No! When this is violated bad luck falls upon those who take rocks home. Many visitors have been known to send rocks back to Hawai'i hoping to reverse all those unlucky things that happened to them.

My Hapa (one of part Hawaiian and part haole/Caucasian blood) heritage has been a mixed blessing. My childhood was at times filled with pain about my mixed/multicultural heritage. I often felt the pain of being on the outside of the mainland culture. Although we spent summers in Hawai'i, I remember experiencing deep emotional pain and separation anxiety when the time arose for our departure from the islands. I cried the entire flight home and I also spent the first week of the school year in tears up until my teen years. I yearned to be back in the land where my brown skin matched the people of my ancestral land. I craved the ending of the school year when I was free to return to Hawai'i where I could dance, sing, swim and play under the sun and rainbows with my brown skinned cousins, aunts and uncles.

Through this sharing and teaching of my elders, I too learned to respect all lands that I have walked upon as sacred. Throughout this book I will share information about journeys and pilgrimages I have taken women to as a teacher and priestess I have embodied this knowledge through the celebration of the Earth's sacred holidays and celebrations, the Solstices and Equinoxes to name a few. The heart of Hawai'i has taught me to love deeply all places I visit and to hear the whispers of the gatekeepers and guardians of those lands.

I teach through a Goddess Community that I formed named Daughters of the Goddess. This is my spiritual home and temple as it is to many women it has served throughout the years. This is now the time of our 16 year anniversary, many moons, prayers and ceremonies have happened since I founded the Temple Summer Solstice 1996. I teach and train the spirit of Aloha to the womyn who circle in Daughters of the Goddess. I don't mean teach in a formalized structured way that this work may evoke. I learned as a young child from my kumu/teachers, kupuna/elders, aunties, and uncles "how to act" as we say in Hawai'i. I model the values, customs and behavior of Hawai'i, of my family, and of our people. Many of the sisters are not of Hawaiian blood, but they uphold this mission of passing on the Aloha spirit, which includes fostering a deep respect and love of the land and the elders.

As I pass on "how to act" to my sisters, the mana/spiritual power I carry within me from the Hawaiian Islands is passed on to each womyn who chooses to circle in DG. In this way, we foster together in harmony the Aloha spirit which all womyn who enter here notice and feel. And you reader will be taught this too.

In Awe of Beauty

In my best of all possible worlds, I live in a tropical rainforest surrounded by endless shades of green, clean water, fresh air and a blazing sun. I have fresh fruit, birdsong and the Timeless Beauty that only Nature can provide.

But in this forest, I have a modern home, fully equipped and furnished. This home is safe, clean, and comfortable.

My nearest neighbor is far enough away for privacy and close enough for kinship. We are different but compatible and our interaction is mutually enriching. There is enough of everything for everyone and no need or desire to harm anyone. We are Primal Life People who are healthy and live in harmony with Nature, Ourselves, and the Spirits---in my best of all possible worlds.

In reality, I live in Oakland California, in a racially diverse neighborhood in a classic craftsmen house. Here there is pollution and homelessness, illiteracy and illness, drugs and violence---a typical urban jungle. I live in this community and I am dedicated to addressing our problems. Fortunately, my work also takes me to many corners of the world.

I have stood silently in awe of the rainforest in Africa, the South Pacific and the Caribbean. I have walked down dusty roads in Mexico and said prayers to the pyramid of the moon. I have watched the volcano erupt and followed Her lava flow to the sea. I've swung from ancient vines in the caves of Jamaica and buried the dead in Dakar. I've danced with delight around totem poles and pressed my forehead to that of Maori warriors. I have eaten strange fruit and wild flowers in Australia and bathed in the waters of the Rhine. I've joked with the pale fox in the crossroads, then wrestled with the Jaguar and won. I have embraced great trees between my thighs; spoke words of love to thunder while riding lightning bolts. I have howled at the moon on the Island of Mu, restored ancient Egypt and dream danced with the souls in Atlantis.

With the help of experience and imagination, I have created a wonderland in my own backyard. There are palm trees and fruit trees, bushy herbs and flowering vines, hummingbirds and butterflies. It is a place where Nature, Humans, and Spirits dance to drum and song. I have created the best forest possible in my world.

Growing Up Down South

Teish's Childhood:

I was born in New Orleans, Louisiana and spent most of my childhood there.

My grandmother and my large family lived in the French Quarters on St. Anne and North Ramparts Streets.

The city of New Orleans is famous for its lush gardens filled with Palmetto palms and Magnolia Grandiflora. It is dotted with marshlands and swamps that produce the red lichen known as Le Baton Rouge on the sides of the trees. Spanish moss hangs in abundance from these trees and would have, in times past, been destined to become baby doll hair and the stuffing for mattresses and pillows.

I enjoyed leaning against a great tree in Congo Square (now Louis Armstrong Park). Congo Square is the place where slaves were auctioned and Mam'zelle Marie LaVeau, the Voudou Queen danced under the moonlight.

This was my environment until I was seven years old.

Then my immediate family moved from New Orleans proper to the West Bank of the Mississippi (the Mother of Rivers) to a small town called Algiers. I started elementary school there. I remember riding the ferry to New Orleans to visit relatives and attend to other important matters. I'd look into the muddy waters of that river, so brown yet so golden in the sunlight and I'd remember the stories of people who'd drowned in a flood, or cast themselves over the sides after losing at games of chance. In a fit of religious ecstasy, others had tried to walk on water and sank deep into the mud. As a child, I had visions of these events and people.

We spent time in several West Bank neighborhoods and finally settled in a small backwoods area called Harvey in Jefferson Parish. We lived in the "Gem Homes, a subdivision for Coloreds." It was the segregated South and "Negroes" were not allowed to live in the same part of town as "Whites". We were one of the first families to move into this area. My family's house sat on a stretch near a babbling brook. The front yard was minimally landscaped with St. Augustine grass, white and yellow daisies, Canna lilies, sunflowers, Seven Sisters Roses and a great Willow tree.

© artwork by Luisah Teish

"I loved this place where all of nature
seemed to perform for me."   Luisah Teish

The land behind the house was so green, so beautiful!

Our land was lush, moist, and fruitful. We had lemon, orange and banana trees. There were blackberry bushes and cow greens, cattails and clover. My favorite place to play was under the willow tree in the front yard. And I used to love to bath in spring and summer rain that fell in 80-degree heat.

The crickets and the frogs sang at night and the fireflies danced in the darkness. Rattlesnakes and cottonmouth moccasins curled up in the blackberry bushes and once in a while some bold alligator would crawl out of the bayou and end up on the dinner table with the crabs and the cornbread. We pulled crawfish from the creeks that ran alongside the house and on special days, we had picnics on the levee and wove hair ornaments, bracelets and belts from the wild clover that grew there.

On hot summer nights my mother would lay a cool sheet on the grass and tell us stories of Brer Rabbit and Brer Fox, about the moon falling in the well, and of the terrifying Pere Malfait who slithered out of the swamps to kidnap bad children who wandered away from home. And most importantly I was taught how to run from snakes and what to do if someone was bitten.

The people in my community had gardens all over the place. Everybody grew something somewhere, or raised chickens, and shared what little they had with each other. I was taught to throw coffee grounds in the garden, and how to harvest sunflower seed from the middle of the blossom. We fried bananas, collected chicken eggs, and grew most of the food we consumed.

I thought the land and the water belonged to us. I enjoyed climbing up on top of the house and looking over the vast expanse of moist green land. It appeared to me that the trees were the nappy hair on the Earth's head. I loved this place where all of nature seemed to perform for me.

Just beyond the subdivision, there was a forest where people built lean- to houses and huts as temporary shelter while they amassed the resources to build something better.

In this neck of the woods, everybody talked in proverbs, worked on the riverfront or in white folks' homes, and had a home remedy for every illness or mental condition. The men fed their dogs gunpowder rolled into ground beef before they left for the hunt.

Then one day a white man came with measuring devices and legal documents. He informed us that we had to put a fence around "our land". Suddenly the land beyond the fence, where I'd played before, now belonged to the "company" and I couldn't go there anymore. I was supposed to suddenly detach from the land and the critters behind the fence because they now belonged to the "company".

"The company " closed off the waterways, cut down the fruit and willow trees, covered the land with stinky mussel shells, and brought in thousands

9

of strange looking pipes that brought "Texas-type" snakes into our environment. I watched an ugly gray building replace the trees and the American flag scarred the skyscape as it blew in the wind.

Along with " the company " came a new message and a new word. Suddenly we were no longer in the "subdivision", now we were in the "suburbs." Now we were supposed to behave differently. There was an encroaching message to give up our "old plantation ways." We were made ashamed of self-sufficiency and told to become "more civilized" consumers. This "plantation shame" still hides in the consciousness of many African-Americans in the North and West.

Many years later, I discovered that "the company" was Exxon and that it had cleaned those ugly pipes with a process, which left radioactive waste on my wonderful land.

At age fourteen, I left my homeland with a group of relatives heading for the West Coast. We drove across country from New Orleans to Palm Springs, California.

As we passed through Texas, I saw Chicanos in the flesh for the first time and realized that these people were far more beautiful than the mockery of them I had seen on television. What I'd seen on television was white men made up to look like "whoever". But when I actually met them I was reminded of people, I knew with last names like Romaine, Dupree and Shoshone, my classmates, and my mother's relatives.

When we came to the Great Mountains (which I'd never seen before), I imagined I saw the spirits of Native Americans embedded in the rocks.

When we arrived in Palm Springs, it was difficult for me to adjust to the dry heat in contrast to the wet, warm, lush green of Louisiana. I suffered Eco-dysphoria and could only amuse myself by speculating about what or who could be under the sand.

After a year of parching in the dry heat, my household was moved to Los Angeles. Now I truly experienced alienation. It was overcrowded (for my spatial sensibility), over-paved, with too many freeways that seemed to make people angry. In addition, I experienced the devastation of the Watts Riots. I remember the National Guard riding down the street, with gun drawn, ready to shoot me as I stood on the front porch of my house. The city felt like a dangerous trash dump. I finished High School there.

I graduated from high school and went to college in Oregon where I was enchanted by the forest but depressed by the never-ending rains and driven underground by falling snow. In the years to come, I lived in the Midwest and visited kindred on the East Coast.

At this point in my life, I have settled (its 38 years at this writing) into an Eco-erotic relationship with the San Francisco Bay Area. I travel to West Africa, Egypt, Central and South America, Austral-Asia, Indonesia and Europe. I have learned to respect the spirits of the land and the people in all of these places. And I enjoy them immensely. However, it is when my plane lands in the San Francisco Bay area that every cell of my body knows that I am home.

I hope that my contribution to this work will help you to experience all of nature as mysterious, beautiful, and worthy of your respect. I hope this work will encourage you to establish a loving and respectful relationship with Mother Earth and Her children. Further, I charge you with the responsibility of preserving and defending them both.

Exercise 1:
First Encounters With the Sacred

What experiences made you aware of sacred space for the first time? What age were you when you first recognized sacred space?

Do you remember the first time you walked into a holy edifice, a cemetery, a reservation, or a village setting? Remember this experience and write about it. Use any form you prefer. It may be poetry, prose, or in letterform. What visual images reflected the sacredness of the place? Doodle, sketch, or draw any images that come to mind.

© Artwork by Luisah Teish

Understand that all of the Forest is Mother Goddess' body,
and we (humans), like the trees in the forest are Her children." Luisah Teish

"Primal Life people experience the forest as a sacred place,
populated with Spirits who are active, receptive, and responsive
to human energy and interaction." Luisah Teish

Chapter Two
The Earth Is Our Mother

The Earth is Our Mother
We must take care of Her (2x)
Hey yunga ho yunga hey yung yung (2x)
Her sacred ground we walk upon,
With every step we take (2x)
The Mother Gives Her Life to us
With every seed we plant (2x)
Hey yunga ho yunga hey yung yung (2x)
The air we breathe is Freedom
With every breath we take. (2 x)
Hey yunga ho yunga hey yung yung (2x)

(Adaptation of a Hopi chant - Ojai Foundation)

The Earth is Our Mother

The song quoted above recognizes that the Earth is Our Mother and must be treated with respect. This belief has been maintained by indigenous peoples' cultures where the Earth is personified as "Mother Earth" and called by many Goddess names: Isis, Asase Yaa, Kali Ma, Gaia and Haumea just to name a few.

Evidence that the people have held onto the feeling of kinship can be witnessed by the fact that children are named after aspects of nature, dependence on the forest is dramatized, and initiatory societies are set up for praising the Earth. Our Mother is honored with practices such as pilgrimages to sacred sites where prayers, blessings and songs are performed in intergenerational circles.

While these attitudes and practices have historically been maintained primarily by country folk, today they are being reawakened and reclaimed by urban dwellers as well. "The Earth is Our Mother" (an adaptation of a Hopi chant) is sung by practioners of neo-paganism (mostly Euro-Americans) and eco-feminist in the WomanSpirit Movement. It is sung on almost every occasion: during New and Full Moon, at the Equinoxes and Solstices, and when performing ceremonies in the open field, on the mountaintop, and on the seashore.

We say that all of Earth is sacred, and further recognize that certain places on this Holy Ground are considered especially so because of particular characteristics.

Now we will examine the Hawaiian and African definitions of sacred lands and discuss the history of a few selected sites. This history will be told primarily through our personal pilgrimage stories. We will share our insights and emotions as well as our ritual actions and social interactions. Through these stories, we hope you will come to love and respect the Earth and the People as much as we do. Most importantly, we will discuss the process of "de-sacralization " and finally make recommendations for "re-sacralizing" our attitude toward the Holy Ground beneath our feet.

Her Sacred Ground

Here we will consider four Hawaiian words relating to the sacredness of the Earth. They are: Hemolele, Ano, La'a, and Kapu.

Hemolele tells us that the Earth is perfect and flawless, naturally. The design of nature is seen as immaculate and in perfect balance. This word speaks of the sacred as yet unaffected by outside (human) influence.

This perfection in nature's design is expressed in the word _Ano_—awe and reverence in the face of nature's beauty. Ano inspires us (humans) to see ourselves as part of the natural landscape and the beauty of Our Mother.

This recognition of our kinship with Mother Earth guides our feelings and directs our behavior toward _La'a_, a devotion to a particular piece of land that has been set-aside for sacred purpose.

Understand that all of the Forest is Mother Goddess' body, and we (humans), like the trees in the forest, are Her children. But it is the beautiful vista of trees, flowers, water, and creatures that inspires us to designate this particular grove as La'a, a place to hold weddings, perform rituals, and give birth to children and culture.

Once designated as La'a we must then observe _Kapu_—specific taboos to regulate human behavior in such as way as to prevent the desacralization of the Holy Ground we stand on.

(Definitions from "Hawaiian Dictionary" by Mary Kawena Pukui)

The Mystical Forest

Primal Life people experience the forest as a sacred place, populated with Spirits who are active, receptive, and responsive to human energy and interaction.

By Primal Life, I mean any group of people who consciously strive to maintain a balanced relationship with Self, Community, Nature, and Spirit. This attitude is inherent in the practices of the African diaspora and other

Eco-Spiritual traditions.

Those of us who are awake can see the growth of plants, hear the song of the wind, feel the movement of the water, and sing with the birds in the trees. We know that nature is active. Some of us petition the Sun, talk to rocks, and receive guidance from the Ancestors in our dreams. We experience the Life Force as receptive and responsive.

Consequently, we practice entering the Forest with caution, reverence, and humility. We enter with caution because we do not imagine that we are "masters of the Earth" with the right to exploit and pillage. Rather we experience this Sacred Zone as a Place with both benevolent spirits (healing herbs and pleasant flowers) and malevolent spirits (bacteria, poisonous insects, and carnivorous animals) who must be placated in order to maintain a balance between these forces. We ask permission to enter and to exit, and we watch for an answer. We do this with reverence by stepping lightly as we walk, by singing songs, and leaving offerings before we take anything. In addition, we recognize that the forest is bigger, stronger, and wiser than we are so we regard it as a powerful Elder and remain humble enough to receive teaching and guidance from the Forest. It is our recognition of the Power of Place that makes Holy Ground, and it is our behavior in the face of awesome beauty that makes us devotees to the Holy Spirit of the Land.

With Every Step We Take

As you will see from the stories that follow, preparation for entering sacred lands is as important as arriving.

Huaka'i—A Sacred Journey

Leilani's Story:

Huaka'i: trip, voyage, journey, mission, procession, parade, to travel.

Our Hula Halau group in San Francisco, CA—Na Lei Hulu I Ka Weiku— The Royal Feathers of the Highest Esteem performed and fundraised for 16 months to prepare for the journey back to the islands. We were scheduled to go in May 2008 and our Kumu Patrick Makuakane had prepared us for this journey through the teachings of the sacred hula and chants of our land. We danced together for 6 years before embarking on this pilgrimage. The huaka'i called us home to see the mountains, valleys, ocean and islands that we spent time learning and dancing about in California. This was not intended to be a tourist excursion. It was rather a place that we would connect to as a community, and pay reverence to through the offerings of our hula, our chanting, our humility and our respect.

This trip would also be of special significance to me personally as my eldest daughter Jade Leilani is also my hula sister. Because this was her senior year in high school, the journey was extra special and a rite of passage for both of us. We started our trip off together from San Francisco Airport sharing laughter, food, and stories as we flew over the Pacific Ocean.

The next morning before sunrise, we greeted the land with respect by going to the sea and having a Kapu Kai - the salt blessing, I share with you at the end of this chapter. We were staying on Waikiki Beach which is one of Hawaii's biggest tourist destinations.

> "The latest affliction of corporate tourism has meant a particularly insidious form of cultural prostitution. The hula, for example- an ancient form of artistic expression with deep and complex religious meaning-has been made ornamental, a form of exotica for the gaping tourist. Far from encouraging a cultural revival, as tourist industry apologist contend, tourism has appropriated and prostituted the accomplishments of a resurgent interest in things Hawaiian (e.g. the use of replicas of Hawaiian artifacts such as fishing and food implements, capes, helmets and other symbols of ancient power to decorate hotels). Hawaiian women meanwhile are marketed on posters from Paris to Tokyo promising an unfettered "primitive" sexuality. Burdened with commodification of our culture and exploitation of our people, Hawaiians exist in an occupied country whose hostage people are forced to witness (and, for many, to participate in) our collective humiliation as tourist artifacts for the First World."
> (From A Native Daughter: Colonialism and Sovereignty in Hawaii. Haunani Kay Trask pg 22-23)

Waikiki was once the beach of our sacred chiefs and royalty, a treasured place in old Hawaii filled with sacred fishponds and taro patches. All of this has been replaced by towering high rises and designer boutiques. As we walked during dawn in silence we passed tourists who had been out all night drinking, some of whom were chatting with high heeled, mini skirt clad, "ladies of the night". I think this is the first time my daughter had seen prostitutes and we all tried to remain solemn and reverent in spite of this disturbing seen. I could not help but feel for the young beautiful sisters I was passing on the street while we made our way to the ocean.

We finally made it to the beautiful ocean, which to me remains holy even in the face of all the tourist development. Holding hands in a circle, we stood waist deep in the waters of the sea. Kumu Patrick had us dip as one unit together in the circle, once for the ancestors, once for the land, once to give thanks, and once to bless ourselves. We returned to our hotel rooms to shower and get ready for the rest of the day.

We rode together in a bus to all parts of the island of O'ahu. We worked in the taro fields and visited with Uncle Butch, a steward of this land. He taught us of the different types of taro and we each had a chance to stand in the rich fertile muddy water filled patches, pulling weeds from around the taro that grows—the food of our Hawaiian people and also our sacred ancestor and parent as well. We all had a good muddy time and washed off afterwards.

We learned of how this valley once rich with rainfall, water and luscious life giving taro patches was practically barren. Water was being diverted from holes drilled into the mountain to support the greenery of golf courses. He talked of tourist places that received the life giving waters from our fertile valleys 'tumors'—as if they were themselves cancerous tumors sucking the life force out of the islands. I felt the devotion and dedication of his service to our islands as he told his story while pounding taro into poi on woven mats in an open-air thatched temple. The wind blew through our hair and kissed our faces as we received the wisdom of this place. He spoke a lot of Hawaiian Sovereignty and justice.

As we left this valley, we were told that the Iolani Palace gates had been locked as sovereignty movement activists were picketing the palace grounds. The Iolani Palace, named after the I'o—the hawk, the bird that soars to the highest places and a symbol of spiritual height. The palace stands on the grounds of an ancient sacred Heiau/temple. The palace was built by King David Kalakaua and was also there during Queen Liliuokalani's reign- our beloved Kupuna and ancestor and last reigning Hawaiian monarch.

Although I have visited the palace several times before this was the first time, my daughter Jade was there. She didn't like being there at all and commented several times about how things just didn't feel right—despite all the grandiosity it possesses—particularly for a creation of it's day.

What I am always most impacted by is the room where our beloved Queen Liliuokalani was imprisoned in for nine months. The room reeks of her heartbreak as our land and our sovereignty were ripped away from her. In 1893 the United States began its illegal occupation of the Hawaiian Islands. Today many people are still demanding justice for this illegal act. As the following quote from Ka Lahui Hawaii, a watchdog association that lobbies for the Federal-State Task Force on the Hawaiian Homes Commission Act, by Haunani Kay Trask demonstrates:

"All groups developed their arguments from the prior existence of the Hawaiian nation, the culpability of the United States in the loss of Hawaiian domain and domination in 1893, the unilateral change in Native citizenship that came with forcible annexation in 1898, and the internationally recognized right of all peoples to self-determination. The specifics of the Native Hawaiian-U.S. relationship had been linked with the universals of the human rights position to form a powerful defense of Hawaiian sovereignty." (Haunani Kay Trask)

In the simplest terms, sovereignty was defined, in the words of *Ka Lahui Hawai'i* as

"The ability of a people who share a common culture, religion, language, value system and land base, to exercise control over their lands and lives, independent of other nations." (Ka Lahui Hawai'i)

In the room, there is a hand stitched quilt that she made displayed in a glass case. She created and stitched this quilt with her own hands believing that she would die in this room. She put into this quilt all of the many emblems and words and stitches of her story.

It communicates strongly her feelings and thoughts of the injustice while also expressing her deep and undying love for this holy land of Hawai'i. It was an invocation to Hawaiian freedom and her message to future generations. The warriors of the land wanted to rise up and fight but she insisted on peace and so her wishes prevailed. While the takeover was seen as 'one of the most successful in US history' because of its absence of war, Liliu felt that one day the children of Hawai'i would have the land returned. That struggle continues.

We left the palace fulfilled and shaken at the same time. Luckily, we were situated at Waikiki Beach where each evening I had my own Kapu Kai—cleansing and releasing all the emotions that were arising during the journey to the sea.

This trip reminds me of my own journey two months earlier where I received my Kahuna Initiation. Auntie Pahia—Kahuna Nui of the islands officiated that ceremony. I was teaching a session at a workshop with Hawaiian elders from the Big Island. As I prepared for this trip, spirit directed me to share the same material I teach while on the continental US. As Uncle Reynolds Kamakawiva'ole said to me in Hawai'i, "this is mainland—our islands. The other place is not the mainland, that is the continental US."

I can't tell you how many times while away from Hawai'i I heard comments such as, "I didn't know Hawai'i had its own language - did you know that?" It is also not common knowledge that the US has been illegally occupying the Hawaiian Islands since 1893. Free Hawai'i bumper stickers from the Koani Foundation are at almost all of the gatherings and classes I teach. A story shared by a woman who had one on her bumper came back to me. She was pulled over by a police officer for something minor—I think a taillight was out. He approached her in a friendly way and while chatting, he asked her about the Free Hawaii bumper sticker. She told him it was in reference to the illegal occupation of the US overthrow of the Hawaiian monarchy. He was surprised by this information and said he thought Hawaii had always been a vacation spot for Americans. And he was serious!

As a woman of Hawaiian ancestry, I had struggled with emotions ranging from anger, depression, rage, and hopelessness. I generally land back at the place of being a bridge in the communication gap of ignorance and misinformation and digging deeply to find the wellspring of compassion.

The Hawaiian word for a Caucasian person is Haole. Many haoles have shared the stories of their deep connection with the islands. Some of them have also experienced prejudice and rejection for being Haole. I know this to be true in my own family, evidence of this perspective can be seen in the culture. As children, we learned that taking what does not belong to you is 'haole style'. It can also mean cold, stingy, unaffectionate, and self-centered. All of these characteristics are seen as 'not Aloha' in Hawaiian culture. As an example, when food is prepared and served for someone "with Aloha" it is given as a gift. Food is sacred as it comes from the Earth and we are taught to be thankful for the abundance we receive. Comments or activities that would indicate dissatisfaction with food in particular are considered ungrateful and rude. Being a picky eater is really not held with high regard and a child growing up in the culture that complains about food can be greeted with a 'good you don't like that –more for us."

My advice to my own children has always been to hold comments on food as praise and thanks and to never make comments about not liking what is given. I also give you this story as a gift to walk gently on the land and to give praise and thanks for those whose ancestors' blood built the places of beauty we now visit.

Homecoming

Original Tapa Cloth

Teish's Story:

Air France flight number "who knows what" landed at the airport in Dakar Senegal in the Spring of 1989. It was the first time I would set foot on African soil. It was the hope of a lifetime manifested.

I was traveling with a small party. There were five of us-three men and two women (myself and my goddaughter Uzuri Amini) and we'd come to Africa with clear purpose, high hopes and open hearts. (As this story unfolds, I will refrain from naming the three men because I no longer have relationships with them).

For decades, I'd envisioned what this moment would look and feel like. I would walk out of the airport into the lush green of my Mother Continent, accompanied by the throbbing of Djembe drums and beautiful people laughing, dancing Funga Alafia and offering me deliciously spiced food locally grown.

In my vision, I would step onto the land, come down on my knees and kiss the Holy Ground before I accepted any of these wonderful gifts.

This had been the dream. The reality was shockingly different.

In reality, my first major accomplishment was surviving the ordeal of customs. The airport was littered with soldiers carrying M16 rifles that they used to rummage through my luggage. We managed to "pay off" the appropriate parties and were ushered out of the airport and into the open air.

I remember a feeling of fear and repulsion overtaking me as I stepped outside. Instead of the throbbing drums and beautiful dancers of my vision, I was greeted with the smell of decaying flesh and the roar of confusion in another language.

The sidewalk was lined, three rows deep, with lepers whose bodies were covered in khaki colored rags and whose faces were covered in sores.

As they stretched out their hands, I saw that many of them had fingers missing. It is a Moslem custom to chop off a knuckle each time a person is caught stealing. Some of these hands were so severely butchered that working or stealing was out of the question. The only thing they could do was beg.

I had changed my American dollars for Senefrancs in the airport and pressed money into as many palms as I could while walking quickly toward a car whose driver signaled us forward and who cautioned me "do not give them money Madame."

The members of my party and I piled into two cars, named our hotel, and began arguing with the drivers about the final cost of the fare.

The driver of my car sped off and maintained a speed of about 90 miles per hour. He drove straight through a marketplace and sent fruit and feathers flying. He almost hit two vendors. I thought this was the opening to a poorly directed adventure movie.

We arrived at our hotel (The Novotel Dakar). I had to bribe the driver into helping me bring the luggage into the hotel lobby. He brought my bags in, dropped them on the floor, collected his money, and ran out the door. The Concierge (A Black Man) walked to the door, looked and came back to me. He said, "That man was your driver?"

"Yes" I answered him. "You paid him?" I said, "Yes". Then he said, "That man is no driver and the car you rode in was stolen at the airport." Before I could react, he handed me a key and said, "Welcome to Senegal Madame."

Vultures in My Window

Well I'd blown the whole "kiss the Holy Ground" scene of my vision. Now all I wanted to do was go to my room, take off my clothes, and wash the scent of lepers off of me. Although one of the men was my husband, we found it more economical to get two rooms, one for the men and one for the two women. Uzuri and I walked into our room and dropped the suitcases on the floor. It was hot and stuffy inside and I sorely needed some fresh air.

I walked over to the window with the intention of opening it but just as I stepped up to it a large black bird, a vulture, slammed itself against the windowpane. I screamed and stepped back from the window. Then I stripped naked, went into the bathroom and scrubbed my body vigorously. When I came out of the shower, I threw myself on the bed and cried myself to sleep.

I did not know it then but the presence of the Vulture was an important omen. Several years earlier I'd been initiated as a priestess of Oshun Ibukole whose animal totem is the African Vulture. I wasn't thinking of that then. I was just in shock. But I realize now that the Vulture is also the

24

Sankofa bird who comes to remind us to fetch the ways of the ancestors and bring them into the future.

I soon came to understand that the Sankofa bird in my window was a fore-shadowing of my coming visit to Goree Island, one of the last doors that many slaves passed through leaving Africa.

LaGoree

The Blood is still in the soil.

The five of us (two African-American women and three men, one black, one Latin, and one white) are following Jared our African guide through the halls of LaGoree, the citadel on an island off the coast of Dakar, Senegal.

Goree Island is known as the "House of Slaves." It was one of the last slave ports to be built off the West Coast of Africa by Dutch invaders in 1776. This is the place where millions of African people were loaded onto slave ships, packed like sardines on their bottom decks, and shipped to the so-called "New World". It is estimated that the rooms of LaGoree held 150-200 people for a period of three months before being deported. The conditions were horrible. There were separate holding quarters for men, women, and children who were held in their cells with limited food and water. The lack of sanitary conditions and the habits of the Dutch caused a pest epidemic as soon as 1779. Young women were kept in special quarters, and their worth was determined by the conditions of their breasts and sexual organs.

Following Jared, we turn down one of the narrow hallways and stop for a second before entering. He tells us that this is "the rape room" and explains how it got this name. It was common practice to bring African men into this room, chained, and make them sit with their backs pressed against the wall. They were forced to watch as the crew of slaveships raped African women en masse. I could still smell it in the soil.

My sister Uzuri, who is very sensitive and intuitive, begins to cry. She has spent many years healing women of the trauma of sexual abuse and knows the pain of it intimately. I tighten my jaw in an attempt to steel and brace myself against the pain.

We step out of that room and as we pass through another narrow hallway I become dizzy and swoon. I imagine that I see myself crouching, hiding maybe, in a hole in the wall. I look at the image of myself. My skin is darker than it is now, my hair is matted and blood runs from a busted lip. The eyes that look at me are both angry and sad but they are--unmistakably--my eyes. For a moment I inhale, my breath gets stuck in my throat. I want to run but can't move. I could hear the screaming in the other room. A hand touches my shoulder. I hear Jared say, "You remember too much, my sister."

His touch and voice bring me back to myself. He explains that this place is "the hole" where they punished "uppity women" who fought back against rape. I see myself in this place and my stomach hurts.

The men in my party are shaking their heads and moaning in shame, anger, and disgust. The impact of what was done here is more than any of us can take. We all stop for a moment, hold hands and breathe. We breathe to gather our strength. We breathe together to re-affirm our kinship. We re-commit to our reason for coming to this place.

Jared leads us to a rectangle of light in the darkness. Now we have come to the Last Door. Stepping left foot first we move single file through the Last Door and stand Oceanside on the rocks. We acknowledge that at a time in the past our presence here could have been very different. The white man would have been ship's captain; the Spaniard, First Mate; and the three black people its cargo.

But today we are here to perform rituals, to offer prayers for the spirits of those ancestors who were sold; to grant forgiveness on the part of sellers, rapists and buyers; and most importantly, to ask that this door be sealed and never used in this way again through the history of humanity. We offer grain and coins, we sacrifice our jewelry, we tuck prayers and poems between the rocks, and we sing and cry. And finally we walk away.

We performed this ritual in Spring, 1989. Today I can still smell the blood in the soil.

Note to the Reader

For accurate information on the history of Goree Island and the slave trade, go to http://webworld.unesco.org/goree. And please ignore the material in

Wikipedia regarding this and other issues of African and African-American history and culture.

The Desacralization Process: Conquistadors on Tour

The moment a foreign power sets its flag upon a piece of land and declares it property, the colonization process begins. This aggressive act was performed in Hawaii and throughout all of Africa. Indeed throughout many places in the world.

Colonization is carried out by "Conquistadors on Tour". They are a band of marauding criminals who rape and pillage in the name of their flag, their supposed superiority and their god. Their methods include demonizing the indigenous deities, outlawing native languages, destroying family and kinship structures and subjecting human beings into servitude and slavery. The conquistadors dig up gold, silver and diamonds, export the fruits and vegetables to foreign lands, and build homes, brothels and churches on top of sacred sites. These are the attitudes and actions that led to the desacralization of land, culture and peoples for hundreds of years (1400s-1900s).

Today we see the attitudes of the conquistadors expressed in the form of Scientific Imperialism. Scientific Imperialism claims that the Earth is the property of man and can and should be exploited for the good of science and human lifestyle requirements. It manifests in deforestation such as the burning of the Amazon Rain Forest to grow alfalfa for hamburger cows. The land in African-American communities is used to bury toxic waste in "brown fields", polluting the air and the water. The bones of Native American ancestors are ripped from their burial grounds and made spectacles in museums, while their sacred salmon and corn are subjected to over fishing and genetic engineering. The shorebirds drown in oil spills, mountains are gutted, and human beings are denied access to clean drinking water. Much of our tourism trade flourishes in an economy based on wage slave labor and human trafficking.

This desacralization is a danger to Life on Earth that is recognized by Primal Life People everywhere.

"The Amazon, Earth's greatest biological treasure, once covered 14 percent of the Earth's surface and now covers only 6 percent. The last remaining rain forests could be consumed in less than forty years. Nearly half the world's species of plants, animals, and microorganisms will then be destroyed or severely threatened, the result of deforestation by multi-national corporations and landowners.

"Lost will be many possible cures for life-threatening diseases. Five centuries ago, ten million Indians lived in the Amazon rain forest. The conquistadors, who came with a cross in one hand and a sword in the other, killed many indigenous peoples and made millions slaves. Today, there are less than two hundred thousand Indians left. Gone are thousands of years of irreplaceable knowledge about the medicinal properties of plants. It is said that each time a shaman or medicine person dies, it is as if a whole library is burning down."

(Grandmother Maria Alice Campos Friere). Grandmothers Counsel the World: Women Elders Offer Their Vision for Our Planet. (Carol Schaefer, editor. Forward by Winona LaDuke pg 74)

This concern is an expressed call for People of Consciousness to stop the desacralization process and to begin the work of re-inspiriting the world. In order to do this we must begin with a shift in our own consciousness.

Wangaari Maathai, the Kenyan environmental activist, and the first African woman to receive the Nobel Peace Prize in 2004 is the Mother of the Green Belt Movement. The women in the movement plant trees to halt deforestation and to organize and empower their lives. In her book "The Green Belt Movement: Sharing the Approach and the Experience", Ms. Maathai says:

"GBM was, however, not only interested in promoting its projects to communities but also aimed at sensitizing them to become custodians of their surrounding environment. Therefore, the overall goal of GBM in Phase 1 was to raise the consciousness of community members to a level that would drive them to do what was right for the environment because their hearts had been touched and their minds convinced-popular opinion notwithstanding."

(Greenbelt Movement. Wangari Maathai pg 33)

Consciousness Change:
Your Right and Your Responsibility

Conquistador Consciousness is borne of colonialism. It is disconnected from Nature and Spirit, and results in the exploitation of animals, plants, minerals, and humans,

In order for people in Western Culture to heal from this condition, several things must be done:

1. Address Western Arrogance:

Realize that you have been miseducated and conditioned out of your natural relationship with Self, Community, Nature and Spirit.

Leilani's example:

Eliminate Feudal Lords. There are landowners who imagine that they are superior to the local and native people of the land. This attitude is followed by actions that oppress the original caretakers of the land and these guardians become slaves and servants to the feudal lords. Learn to respect the land and the people.

Teish's example:

Intellectual Imperialism. There are Ph.D. students who "interview" the indigenous elders and drain their brains for information that was sacred, centuries old and unknown to the student beforehand. They take copious notes and then write their thesis and a popular book without acknowledging the elder, and without monetary compensation. Further, these intellectual midgets take license to change not only the history, but also the knowledge and slant it toward a Euro-centric view of superiority. Stop it please.

2. Release Past Conditioning:

Prepare to let go of your past conditioning, agree to do no harm, and seek new knowledge from respected elders.

Example ~ Teish and Leilani:

Examine Your Sense of Entitlement:

Is the wealth of your family based on the past exploitation of others? Are you heirs to a slave master's legacy? How does this manifest as "privilege" and how does it cause you to treat others? Perhaps you grew up viewing Native American bones in the museum without ever realizing the desecration of those graves. Are you wearing blood diamonds from the African diamond underground? Do you feel any sense of responsibility toward stopping that business? Do you make sure that your housekeeper is a woman of color and is she underpaid and under appreciated? You must examine yourself in these regards.

Commit To Do No More Harm:

Was nature seen as an integral part of your play and world? What has your connection been to the forest, trees, rivers, streams and ocean? If you grew up in a concrete jungle or a glass tower, you must change your relationship to the natural world. Stop polluting the Earth, reduce your carbon footprint as much as your life will allow. Explore where your food comes from. Is what you are eating for dinner the product of de-forestation or over fishing? Are you destroying the world's air currents in exchange for a $1.00 hamburger? Clean up any language you use that implies inequality or disrespect of others. Seek new knowledge from elders respectfully. Come with gifts and a reasonable amount of humility. Be unassuming as you ask the elder what they feel you might be able to learn.

3. Re-evaluate Western Economics:

Realize that the almighty dollar is not God. Commit to balanced relationships with Nature, the Human Community and the World of Spirits.

Leilani's Example:

Learn to value all services and benevolent acts given to you. Do not assume what you have received is FREE. In many cultures, it is inappropriate to ask for monetary exchange and the assumptions are that you will make an offering of equal value. When you go to someone's home to share a meal always offer to help clean up afterwards with the sincere intention to do so.

I have found myself sometimes in a spontaneous situation where I did not know I was going to receive the gift of wisdom, hospitality, etc. So I gave a piece of jewelry or the scarf I had on as a gift. We must learn to value gestures of giving and thanks over ownership of material possessions.

Teish's Example:

Prepare to sacrifice, to make sacred your acts of gift giving, and practice mutually beneficial exchanges with humans, nature and spirit.

Once I was called in to mediate a dispute between an African man and a Euro-American woman who had gone into business together. She felt that he owed her money for the electric bill. He pointed out that at a time of crisis he had buried her father at his own expense, conducted the funeral and continued to say prayers and perform rituals for the father's soul. She did not understand his valuation of spiritual currency. For him these ritual acts could not be compared to monetary transactions as they were of great value. She placed her primary value on money. To make her understand I converted his actions into wage hours for a psychiatrist, funeral parlor director, and parish priest. It was, of course, absurd because the heart felt work is worth more than a simple money transaction.

4. Recover Your Indigenous Mind:

Here Leilani and I offer you a few attitudes and actions that you can incorporate into your life that will facilitate the recovery of your Being.

Teish's Recommendations:

Realize that Spirit is embodied in the world, and that Nature and the Earth are sacred. Your personal destiny is interconnected with everyone and everything. Focus on Community, collective balance and health. The concept of community extends beyond death. Hold reverence for the elders, the ancestors and the unborn. Practice the ethics of integrity, personal responsibility and accountability to the community, rather than working from a place of sin, guilt, and punishment. Demonstrate reverence for the cycles of birth, growth, death and regeneration. Focus on ritual, ceremony, vision and direct experience rather than dogma and the tyranny of text. Do not proselytize. Realize that every tradition has experienced repression and resisted it to survive. The circle is sacred, find your place in the circle and move around it with grace.

Leilani's Recommendations:

Participate in community events that involve Earth-based spirituality. Get a reading from a local diviner or ritualist. Give back a donation to the native people whenever you travel and continue to do so throughout time as long as the memory of what you received from this place lasts.

The Rituals

Hawaiian Salt Blessing:

I often use this blessing when entering a new place and also when I am traveling and need extra connection to the spirit of the place I'm visiting. A ritual act called Kapu Kai is done in Hawai'i when we prepare for ceremony. We make a pilgrimage to the sea, bathe in the healing salt waters of the Hawaiian Ocean, and ask that we be blessed and cleansed. We are freed and released of any "old" energies from the past that would not serve the higher good of our lives.

I am going to share with you a modified version of this blessing when we are unable to access the waters of the healing Hawaiian ocean. You will need sea salt, a small bowl and some tap water. The intention you hold is the most important ingredient for this blessing. I usually fill the bowl halfway with water, sprinkle some of the salt inside, and pray over the water. While holding the bowl with one hand and holding my other hand near the water saying words such as, " Please bless this water with all the power of the ocean, the land and help of the Hawaiian ancestors. Allow all those things that I no longer need to be released and bring forth those energies that best support me for my higher good and the good of those around me".

I then put my fingers in the water and touch my forehead, neck, heart— anywhere that I feel would like this healing. I then thank the water for bestowing this blessing and offer the water back to the Earth or dirt, careful not to put the salty water on a plant. Take a deep breath and feel the blessing of the sea. Please feel free to perform this healing blessing at the beginning of a sacred journey and any time you feel the need for this during your stay on the land. You can also use this blessing as part of your spiritual practice at home to keep your connection to the land respectful and whole.

The Sacred Grove: A Guided Visualization

Ago Elegba, Master of the Crossroads
Ago Ogun, Lord of the Forest
Ago Ochossi, Caretaker of the Land
Open the way and clear a path for me.
Hear me as I sing your praises.
Let me step lightly,
Guide and direct my feet.
Ase, Ase, Asese O

(Prayer to the Ebora before entering the Forest, Luisah Teish)

The scenery is green. It is as many shades of green as your mind can imagine as many shades of green as you have ever seen in your entire life. Place yourself in a green forest, surrounded by trees and leaves, vines and flowers, bushes and herbs. Feel the warmth of the Sun caressing your face, or gently gracing the nape of your neck. In the distance, the sound of water can be heard. It may be the ocean, the river, or rain trickling down into a stream. Inhale. Do you smell the scents of plumeria, of cinnamon, verbena or banana? Let the wind enter your nostrils, fill your lungs with the breathe of the Earth, moist, warm, air wraps itself around you carrying your scent in the mixture, running pollen through your hair, cooling the beads of moisture on your skin. Follow that gentle breeze through the trees or across the mountain. Dip briefly into the cave. Wet your feet in the cool clean water. Pick something bright and sweet to eat.

Step with care as you walk through the forest. Be sure not to trample the leaves beneath your feet. Listen well for the song of the birds, and the scratching sounds of the insects in the trees. Listen even more carefully for stealthy hisses, low guttural growls, and the approaching thunder of pounding hooves.

Look at yourself in this vision. See the color of your skin, the texture of your hair, your body adorned with pigments, feathers and hide. Know that you are home there, that you belong there. Take your place in the scenery, watching all that is around you. And know that you are being watched by all that is unseen.

For now, the curtain is open and we can move gracefully between the worlds.

Saluting the Land:
The Sacred Sites Chart

This chart briefly illustrates the relationship between the Deities of the Hawaiian and African Diasporas, Their sacred places, elements and objects, and Their attributes.

In both traditions it is customary to address, by prayer and song, the Spirits of the Place in Nature that you wish to enter, cross over, or walk through.

The Sacred Sites Chart

Attributes /Ceremony	Elements/Objects & Symbols	African Deity	Sacred Places Totem	Hawaiian Deity	Element Object Symbol	Attribute Ceremony
Chance, Protection, Trickery, Choice, Guidance	Stones, Sticks, Arrows, Tools of Iron, Lead, Material culture	The Ebora: Elegba, Ogun Ochossi	Crossroads, Doorways, Bushes, Pathways	Maui	Fish hook	Trickery, Discovery
Humility, Wisdom, Courage, Civilization, Justice, Humility	Light and Fire, Pyrite, Pewter,	Olorun, Obatala, Shango	Sky, clouds, Mountains, Thunderstorms	Kanehekili Lono Wakea	Thunder, White cloth, Taro	Prosperity, Peace, Cosmic, Lineage
Strength, Virility, Medicine, Prosperity, Material evolution	Great Trees, Herbs, Fruit and Grain	Osayin, Orisha Oko, Iroko	Forest, Garden, Open Field	Laka Haumea/Papa Elepaio	Ferns, Land, Fertile Soil, Food, Birds, taro	Hula, Lei making, Canoe building
Passion, Vitality, Change and Transformation	Lava flow, Earthquake, Hurricane, Tornado	Oya, Aganju,	Forest, Volcano, Cave, Cemetery	Laka Pele Hi''iaka	Flowers, Ferns, Lava flow	Healing, Passion, Transformation
Sensuality, Fertility, Beauty, Art and Culture	Sweet Flowing Water, Earth, Flowers, Ferns	Oshun, Mami Wata, Olosa	Rivers, Lakes, Streams, Forest, Waterfall	Hinakuluiau	Greenery, Wood, Yellow	Rain-Making, Flow of Water
Mystery, Nurturance, Women's crafts	Salt Water, Sea Creatures	Olokun, Yemaya, Asupa	Deep Ocean, Ocean waves, Moon	Hina	Taro, Moon, Tapa cloth, Mulberry Tree-bark	Adornment, Women's refuge, Safety

We will now give you a brief overview of the information contained in the chart. This is done to increase your overall understanding of the Eco-Spiritual system. As you read each paragraph know that these descriptions are provided to introduce you to the Deity who personifies that place in Nature, and to help you see yourself in that place, as a child of that Deity.

Later in this chapter, we will provide a few rituals for the Deities to demonstrate how the material is integrated. While we encourage you to perform the very simple rituals provided here, we also advise you to attend our workshops. There we will share our knowledge and experience, and teach you how to design and orchestrate many more rituals with reverence and good results. Later in this work travel opportunities are discussed.

In the African tradition, Elegba, Ogun and Ochossi, the Ebora, are addressed first. We salute Them and ask their permission to enter. We also ask for their guidance and protection as we travel. Elegba is the linguist of the Deities; He translates our human language into a vibrational one that can be understood by the Forces of Nature. Ogun clears a path so that we may find our way. He removes both the external and internal obstacles that could impede progress. Ochossi provides us with the skills we need in order to survive and thrive as we journey through this life.

So, for example, if you wanted to enter a cemetery, you would invoke the Ebora and receive permission to enter. Then you would sing, and make an offering to Oya as you petitioned Her to bring about Transformation in your affairs.

Similarly, if you wanted to approach the Volcano in Hawaii, you could invoke Maui and give thanks for the existence of the Islands then say a prayer to Pele as you make an offering.

The Deity being approached and the request being made will determine each prayer and offering. We will provide information that is more specific in our Sacred Sites Etiquette Workshops.

For now, it is sufficient to say that in every instance what remains important is that you ask permission, address the Deity humbly, make offerings, state your case or concern, listen carefully, and feel deeply for the response as you take your leave with gratitude.

And most importantly, leave the place in the condition you found it at least. However, if the Place has been desacralized we hope you will be inspired to pick up trash, care for creatures and people, build roadside altars, and commit other acts to re-establish Holy Ground.

The Eco-Spiritual Chart Explanations

Gatekeepers:

Teish:

Elegba, Ogun, and Ochossi are the Warrior Deities who open the road and clear the path. They can be found at openings such as the doorways of a house or temple, the crossroads of city streets and at those places where civilization gives way to entry into the wild.

Their emblems are foundation stones, fighting sticks, the bow and arrow and the iron tools of material civilization. Their colors are red and black (Elegba) green and black (Ogun) and green and brown (Ochossi). They provide guidance but may also be associated with trickery, ironic humor, and human misperception.

These deities should be saluted before entering the forest, when dealing with animals, and in any endeavor that calls for stealth and stamina. Offerings are made to them in multiples of three: three stones, nine arrows, or 21 pennies. We always ask them to "Be Cool".

Leilani:

Maui is the trickster who pulled the Hawaiian Islands up from the Ocean floor, and who is the son of the Moon Goddess Hina. As a navigational expert, He went forth on a journey of discovery over the vast ocean to bring forth the Hawaiian Islands. He is the bringer of new quests for knowledge and new ways beings. He is the great adventurer who is also the devoted and loving son to Hina during his rest periods. He is associated with the fishhook and the island of Maui is named after him. He has a wonderful sense of humor. He was a respectful traveler of lands near and far who brought joy and reverence to all places and peoples he visited. Think of

Maui during your travels to new lands as a gatekeeper of walking with right/ pono action. Pay particular attention to him when your journey takes you across the ocean.

Sky Beings

Teish:

Olorun is the Owner of the Sky, the beautiful blue background against which Obatala rests. Oba-tala means "King of the White Cloth", the clouds and the Light of Heaven. Whereas Olorun is regarded as somewhat aloof, resting high in the heavens, Obatala is envisioned as a Benevolent Father Who created the continents and Who shapes the child in the womb. He is old, wise, and peaceful. His colors are all shades of white with touches of purple, silver, orange and red. His number is eight and the mountaintop is His resting place.

Shango is the Lord of Thunder, the Great Booming Voice of Justice and the Fire of the Human Spirit. He is envisioned as a virile, hot-tempered force with undying courage and ravenous appetites. He is the consort of Oya and, as Thunder and Lightning, they provide the release of atmospheric tension in a tropical storm. Shango's colors are red and white, his number is six and the double-headed axe is His dance wand.

Raise your arms to the sky, take a deep breathe and release it in hardy laughter and know that Obatala will provide you with humility and Shango will make you courageous enough to mingle with other humans as kindred spirits.

Leilani:

Lono, Kanehikili, and Wakea are beloved sky deities that govern the sky realm. Wakea is sky father husband of Earth Mother Papa-Haumea. Wakea is the light of the Sun that opens the door of the Sun. Through their union comes the first child or ancestor of the taro. Kane is also a deity of procreation who is the ancestor to chiefs and commoners. The many faces of Kane also appear as Kanehekili God of Thunder. There is an association with Obatala and Shango.

Lono gives us the cloud signs and prophecies through thunder, rainbows, dark clouds, gushing springs, and rain. Associations with Lono are the red and white fish, the black coconut, awa and the food gourd covered with wicker. Prayers are said before mealtime over the gourd. Lono's season is between the months of October and February and the rising of the Pleiades, which also begins the Makahiki Festival that heralds a time of peace, prosperity and feasting. They would be honored through approaching travels by taking time to pray to the sky and open yourself to meditation and your heart to peace.

Forest, Field and Volcano

Teish:

The environment of the Forest is the most sacred place in the mythology of the African Diaspora. It is populated with Deities possessing amazing powers and wonderful personalities. Truly every tree, mountain and field is viewed as being imbued with Ase, the power of Life. Here we will consider a few of them namely Osayin, Orisha Oko, Iroko, Aganju, and Oya.

Iroko is the beloved African Oak tree. It represents the strength and intelligence of the trees in the forest that stands for hundreds of years bearing witness to human activity and providing air, seed, and habitat to many creatures.

Osayin is the deity of the wild herbs in the Forest. He is seen as a man with one-eye, one arm, and one leg Who can see better, do more, and dance faster than anyone else. Osayin bespeaks our reverence and dependence on the herbs to heal us.

Orisha Oko is the Deity of Agriculture, the one responsible for the art and science of farming. Through Oko, we are able to identify the leaves, fruit, tubers and berries that nourish and sustain us and the ways to grow them and provide for generations to come.

Aganju is the tempestuous Father of Shango, the magma, and the hot lava in the belly of the Volcano. Aganju enriches the soil with volcanic ash, clears the air and carries us across turbulent waters. Aganju is a relative of Pele, the Hawaiian Goddess of the Volcano. When Aganju erupts and His lava flows to the Ocean He mates with Yemaya and They create New Land.

<u>Oya</u> is the weather in its most tumultuous forms. She is the earthquake, hurricane, tornado, and lightning storm. She is the Wild-woman in the woods, the Queen of the Winds of Change and the Boss Lady of the Cemetery. We see Her in the horns of the Cape Buffalo and the dance of the wide-eyed deer. She wears a necklace of nine human skulls and Her skirt contains all the colors of the rainbow.

This conjunction of Deities embodies all the manifestations of Life in the Tropics and They must be respected for Their importance and Their support. Do not imagine that you can enter a tropical forest until you have asked permission and been granted admission. Then be sure to step lightly and to give thanks for Their very existence.

© **Graphic by Jade Sussenguth**

Leilani:

As we journey towards the Earth realm, the Goddesses of Hawai'i call to us. We see <u>Laka</u> Goddess of the Hula dancing with ferns and flowers, wind through Her hair and misty dew covering Her skin. She is sacred dance, nature in motion, and prayer embodied. The maile is sacred to Her. Call to Laka to embrace your beauty and to develop a deep love and Aloha for nature and the land/Aina.

Gifted by all the suppleness of the abundance of nature Her mother Haumea-Papa the fertile Earth fills Her body with fruits and flowers of the Earth. Haumea is Goddess of prosperity and abundance. She provides food, sustenance, and plenty to the land. Give back generously to loved ones and places you visit to receive Her deepest blessings. Haumea provides the trees for canoe builders from the forest as <u>Elepaio</u> chirps to the harvesters to find the right tree. Elepaio is the sacred bird Goddess who manifests as a strong tree to be crafted into a canoe for safe ocean voyages and harvesting food from the sea.

<u>Pele's</u> favored younger sister <u>Hi'iaka</u> travel safely to Hawai'i from Kahiki while younger sister is held as an egg cuddled under Her arm near Pele's breast. Hi'iaka is also aid to Pele in later years as she accesses Pele during her times of deep trance. The red lehua blossoms of the Ohia tree are sacred to Pele and it is said that if you pick one during your trip to visit Her at the volcano you will bring rain. Pele Goddess of the volcano, fire, passion, deep transformation, charges you to release all that no longer serves you to the Fire of truth and to live your passion. Dance the Fire of Sacred Truth to free your deepest desires.

Sweet Water

Teish:

<u>Oshun</u> is the Goddess of Love, Art, and Sensuality. She is the moisture of the forest. The undulating River is Her dancing body. Her streams cool the planet, the ferns and the flowers are graced with morning dew.

She is unsurpassed as a healer. When the doctor fails, Oshun heals with plain water. She brings sexual pleasure, fertility and happy healthy children

41

to those who bathe in Her waters.

She has a reputation as "the Generous Mother" who gives Her love to everyone. At one time Oshun owned all the jewelry, all the music, and the feathers of the beautiful birds, but She gave them away so She could see Her own beauty reflected in the mirror of Her sister's eyes. She is sister to Oya--the Niger River, to Mami Wata the Waterfall, and Olosa the Lake. She is daughter to Yemaya--the Ocean and Orunmila the Diviner of Destiny is Her consort.

She is the Magical Muse. Human beings who are inspired to create beauty have been kissed by Oshun.

Give praise and thanks to Oshun when you fall in love, pick a flower, or drink a glass of water. Be kind to women and children as a tribute to Her. Sing, write, dance and make love but also pick up trash, avoid over fishing and defend the water rights of all people as a tribute to Oshun and the Sweet Waters of the World.

Leilani:

Hinakuluiau brings forth the sweet rains to the land, Her plants and children. Rain magic is done to Her during times of drought and when fresh waters are needed. She also works along with the clouds of Lono to bring forth wetness. There are over 200 Hawaiian words to describe the different kinds of rain. In song and hula, rain can also be used as a metaphor to express many emotions. Joy, growth, life, greenery, and good fortune, the presence of deities or royalty, sexual relations, and beauty can be associated with light rains. Heavy rains are often used to symbolize grief, sorrow and tears. Allow Hinakuluiau into your emotional self to feel deeply the spirit moving through you. Drink deeply.

The Moon and the Tides

Teish:

The Moon looms high and full overhead. Her light shines on the Ocean. They dance with the tides Asupa (the Moon) and Yemaya (the Ocean).

Asupa guides the flow of moisture on the Earth as She changes from Full to Dark to New. Yemaya's waves rush and hum as She regulates the behavior of the fish in the sea, the child in the womb, and even the formation of the clouds in the sky (Obatala). When light touches the water life stirs in Her womb. Yemaya's colors are blue and silver. Her number is the mysterious Seven. She is the Mother of Secrets and the Keeper of Our Dreams.

And far below the surface, we dive into the watery depths of Olokun Who dwells at the bottom of the Sea. No one knows what's at the bottom of the Ocean and the gender of Olokun is a controversy unresolved. But fall into the deep sleep of the unconscious or reach for the forgotten knowledge of the Ancient Ones, there you will encounter the Castle of Olokun.

Touch a pregnant belly and praise Yemaya. Salute Olokun to awaken from a deep sleep. Step into the salt water and bathe yourself in Moonlight. Give thanks for your birth and that of the planet eternally.

Leilani:

Look to the full moon above the ocean, see Her reflection in the sky, Her light upon the water and give thanks to Hina our 'woman in the moon'. She lived amongst the village for many years working hard to be a good wife and provide the best and finest tapa in the land. She would grow the mulberry tree until the bark could be harvested for the rich moist inner bark that becomes cloth for sleeping mats and bedding, clothes and altar clothes.

Hina worked from the time morning start appeared in the sky until evening star would appear at night. Pounding the bark into soft supple cloth with the tapa beater takes many hours and sometimes days. Beautiful dyes from Her native plants give the cloth an extra flair of artistic genius. Patterns symbolizing the sky, earth, ocean voyages and family lineage all are dyed upon the tapa cloth. Hina lives on the moon, as Her refuge from complaining husbands, family and village members. When Hina knows She has given enough, She climbs the moon, the rainbow of liberation, and sets Herself free. Call Hina into your life when you need respite and comfort from life's toils and to open your inner artist.

© Artwork by Luisah Teish

The Goddesses and Their Rituals

Yemaya: Respecting the Water

Yemaya Asesu
Asesu Yemaya (2x)
Yemaya Olodo
Olodo Yemaya (2x)
(Traditional Yoruba song for Yemaya)

Anywhere the salt waters of the Ocean touch the shores we feel the presence of Yemaya, The Great Womb of the World.

All over the planet and through all times humans have recognized and respected the powers of the Ocean. She provides water for the rain clouds; She provides fish for food and shells for jewelry. Her depths and waves allow us to move from one continent to another.

There are customs, and rituals of giving back to She Who Nurtures Us All.

For example:

During the Winter season between December 21 and Jan 1, rituals are performed to petition the Ocean for blessings and to adorn Her with lovely gifts. In Ghana, Togo, and Benin the children of Mami Wata cast themselves into the sea to re-enact our marine beginnings in the womb. In South America Brazil is known for its midnight offering to Imanje. On New Year's Eve, millions of devotees (mostly women) dress in their finest white clothes. They process down to the beaches of Rio de Janeiro and Bahia carrying bouquets of flowers and balancing small boats on their heads. The boats are crafted from banana and palm leaves and are loaded with flowers, beads, sweets, and coins. The people anchor candles in the sand and light them placing their offering boats at the sandy edge of the sea. Then they play drums, sing and dance, invoking and enticing the Great Mother of the Waters to come and receive Her gifts. And She responds by sending a great wave that always arrives at midnight, to overtake the offerings and wash them out to sea. This happens every New Year's Eve night. It has happened this way for centuries.

Whereas the beaches in Brazil and Ghana are adorned with banana boats and flowers, far too many of our shorelines are littered with garbage and scarred by oil spills. Before we can create rituals and institute culture we must halt the devastation and resacralize the land. This is best done with "house cleaning sessions".

Housecleaning

1. You can go down to the shore with a garbage bag and a sharp stick and pick up paper, cans and plastic and recycle them appropriately.

2. Avoid using plastic. Every piece of plastic ever made still exists. Lots of it is ending up in the ocean, in the intestines of fish eaten by shorebirds and humans. We cannot throw anything away – because there is no "away". Use plates and glasses made of natural substances and wash dishes using non-toxic soap.

3. Be aware of what you eat. Most spiritual traditions have food taboos,

45

and various schools of health recommend specific diets. Those who have embraced vegetarian and vegan diets have a different set of concerns. Many people who are averse to red meat and the hormones found in some poultry rely on seafood for their nutritional needs, and culinary cultural identity (New Orleans Seafood Gumbo for example). Those of us who want to honor Yemaya with a seafood feast, yet are concerned about the environment, have several important facts to take into consideration:

4. Limit your consumption of shrimp! Shrimp are at the low end of the food chain. Trawling for shrimp nets all of their natural predators: fish, sharks, dolphins, and turtles. For every pound of shrimp on your plate, ten pounds of dead "bycatch" gets ground-up and thrown back into the ocean.

5. Avoid eating farmed Shrimp! Farmed shrimp is a chemical-intensive industry that that depends on clear-cutting thousands of hectares of mangrove wetlands. Antibiotics are poured into the waters until the area can no longer support life. Then the farm is moved to another area.

6. Avoid eating farmed Salmon: The Salmon is sacred to Native North Americans. They believe that Creator provided the Salmon to remind us on land, of our connection to the sea. This is similar to the African belief about the bearded Black Catfish. The fish farming industry employs practices that contaminates the fish and destroys the food supply needed by the Wild Salmon. Salmon is regarded as the most beneficial for human consumption and highly endangered. We can show gratitude to Yemaya and the Native Spirits by respecting and revering the Salmon.

7. Recognize the sacredness of food: It is often said that "you are what you eat". When you consume a meal, you take the life energy of the "beings on your plate" (including the grains and vegetables) into your physical and spiritual bodies.

8. It is important to know the fish you are eating. Some fish are healthy and have short life cycles so they do not accumulate our chemical toxins. Some fish are "top predators" and contain bio-concentrate pollutants like mercury and insecticides. Know the fish you eat. Some fish come from robust populations, many are over-fished or are taken by drag trawling, long lining, and other deadly wasteful fishing practices.

9. Sit quietly on the shore and ask Yemaya what gift She would like from

you. Here are a few possibilities: (A.) A donation to a shelter for women and children. (B.) Keeping a dream journal. (C.) Re-educate ourselves to incorporate "mindful behavior".

Example: A child collecting seashells for a science class will collect without consideration for the seashore. She is concerned about her grade and the teacher does not develop ecological awareness nor spiritual sensitivity. The remedy in this case would be to collect only one example of each shell, and to compensate with ritual and work. Here the child should make an offering to Yemaya by picking up trash from the seashore, and making a money contribution to the mother's milk bank. In this way, the child would have a holistic understanding including conservation, spirituality, and social responsibility. In this way, the child would heal herself through a change of habit, revere the Earth and Spirit through ritual and work, and have a positive impact on society through her contribution.

However, let me state what is most important.

The Ocean is much too large and way too complicated for us to fully understand. However, you must remember that we are all born in a bowl of saltwater (the placenta) and recognize that She is the Mother of Us All. She loves and provides for us. But you must respect and care for the water by using Her resources--the fish, the medicine and the jewels- in right proportion. Commit to acts of kinship and kindness in Her name, and embrace Her Mystery through meditation and ritual.

Haumea: Permission To Pick Plants

Talk to me mama Haumea
sacred forest, flowers, plants
and herbs of healing and food.
Do I have your permission to enter the forest?
Have I prepared properly,
grounded and centered
enough to receive the holy plant ancestors
from our ohana/family, our parents?

(Leilani Birely)

47

Leaves of the maile vine that grow deep in the forest on treetops, beloved ferns growing underneath the canopy of koa trees, grant me the honor of receiving you. Ohia trees and lehua buds of the volcano, may I have your flowers as an offering to my altar, my leis, my medicinal potions, and my food?

Chanting or praying before picking sacred plants is common practice to our Hawaiian ways. Clearing the mind of idle chatter and the troubles of our week or day helps open us to hearing the messages and songs of the plant ohana/family that offer themselves to our sacred work. Begin at the entrance of the place you want to gather and offer a prayer. The prayer can be simple or elaborate but most of all an open heart, mindfulness, respect and reverence are necessary intention ingredients. Here is a prayer that I will share:

Oh Blessed and Sacred Forest
I, Leilani come to you Haumea Earth Mother with the
intention of pono/right action. Please allow me to receive
the gifts you have to offer. Allow my ike/psychic
sight to be open and clear so that I may know
and hear all the seen and unseen messages.
E HO MAI--Bring this energy towards me.
Mahalo Nui Loa Akua Wahine
Thank you very much Goddess
(Leilani Birely)

Our plant family will speak to us with the help of the elements. The plant to be harvested will often identify itself to you by blowing in the wind or waving to you. A branch or leaf may appear on the path. Take note of all the ways She is speaking to you and sharing the gifts offered.

Do not despair if you do not see any of these signs. Often, this can be read as an indication that we must start again. I have heard of kahuna lapa'au-- herbal Hawaiian medicinal healers, who having had this experience realized that they needed to go back to the entrance, to pray and ask permission again.

All things from nature must be asked permission to see if they want to participate in our human endeavors. We are in a collaborative relationship

48

with nature and our position is to take Her lead. If the answer is 'no' and something does not want to be offered, please respect this boundary with humility and move on.

Oya: Feeding the Wind

Iba Oya
Iba Yansa
Ayaba won obinrin
Mo be yin

Ajalaiye fun Alafia
Ajalorun fun ire
Oya Yansa fun ire
Oya Yansa wini wini
Ase Ase Ase

Praise to the spirit of the wind
Oya the Mother of Nine.
Queen of the Women
Save us, Save Us
Winds of the Earth bring Health
Winds of the Heavens bring Fortune
The Wind Mother is Wondrous

It is so, so be it, so it is.
(Luisah Teish)

Softly a whistle rises in the wind, gently the dust broom sweeps. Leaves rustle against the Earth. She rises, growing stronger, standing taller, pushing farther, yielding more. Oya, Queen of the Winds of Change.

Long and swift, She dances through our lives, hurling lightning, spitting fire, as furiously torrential rains fall. We reap the harvest; we grab the shafts of wheat and rip them from the soil. Oya, Mother of Transformation, we work so well for Her.

Lady of the Sunset. It is She who paints the leaves in autumn; the hum of locusts is Her song. Her nine heads, the River Niger are adorned with a necklace of human heads. There in the cemetery She dances among the tombstones with Her Sisters at Her side. There in Her garden leaves and seeds fly; rain falls upon the Earth. Death and Life rustle in the Wind, the seasons change and we who are Dead reborn must worship Her.

The Goddess Oya is the Queen of the Winds of Change. She is the Wild woman in the Woods, the archetype of unconditional change in Nature. She is the Lady of Transformation, the agent of change in human life; and the Boss Lady of the Cemetery who oversees the Great Change, the return to the spirit world. This Goddess appears in some form in every culture on the globe. For everywhere humans live with the weather, are born, mature, and die... this is the natural and inevitable cycle of change. The Mother of Change is feared and greatly revered. We have already discussed some of Her attributes in the chart. But now we come to Her to ask for cleansing, healing and assistance. We come to Her prepared to release ourselves from the debris swirling in the dust devils of our existence. And we come to Her prepared to be the agents of the change we seek.

It is a beautiful day in Autumn. Strong winds blow the leaves.

Choose an open field during Fall in order to catch a strong wind.

Choose a place where the local birds feed.

Purchase a large bag of wild birdseed.

For nine days, stir the seeds in a counterclockwise motion

Asking Oya to change negative effects such as:

1. Global warming
2. Childhood Sexual Slavery
3. Mental Illness
4. War and Social injustice
5. Economic Hardship
6. Exploitation of Animals
7. Blocked creativity
8. Conquistador Consciousness
9. Fear of the Mysteries.

Breathe in your commitment to change by working to:

1. Protect the environment
2. Liberate the children of the world
3. Provide aid and assistance to someone in mental distress
4. Stand up for justice and peace
5. Practice wealth-sharing
6. Protect endangered species.
7. Fully embrace your creative abilities and support local artists
8. Become a conscious traveler
9. Learn to embrace Mystery.

Go to the open field and take nine slow deep breathes.

Dance in clockwise circles as you throw hands full of the birdseed into the air current, watching as it lands on the ground.

As the birds come to feed, talk to them and ask them to take your prayer to the Wind Mother, Oya.

Ask Her to help you make important changes in your life. For the next nine days make note of the ideas that occur to you and the people and opportunities that present themselves.

Pele: Dancing for the Fire

E Pele E Pele E
Sweet flowing Mother Earth,
hot molten lava,
bringer of new Earth
and destroyer of old,
Share your passion
your commitment
and courage to dance
and speak the fire of sacred truth.
(Leilani Birely)

Fire as truth, fire as passion, fire as creativity...Light a candle in Her name and ask for all these attributes. Go outdoors or stand in front of a mirror. Gently swing your hips side to side, breathing in the life force, the fire of life. Allow the spine to open up, the pelvis, and the lower back. Feel the flow of the Earth's energy rise up through your feet, into your calves, knees, thighs, hips, spine, belly organs, chest, heart, shoulders, throat, head, face, spreading out the arms and fingertips.

Feel the healing beat of the Earth's core warm your body and soul. If your eyes have been closed, open them and look into the flame of your candle. Let a soft gaze rest upon the light and speak your truths out loud or silently. Ask for those things you want to draw strength upon and call into your life and those things that no longer serve you that you would like to release. Reach your hands to the sky waving them side to side feeling that you are dancing and fanning the fire of your desire.

Exercise 2:
Overcoming Conquistador Consciousness

Review the materials presented in this chapter. Then examine the ways that you have been mis-educated into Conquistador Consciousness. Make a list of its effects on your life and your relationship to the Earth and other people. Consider the efforts you have made to overcome it and evaluate their effectiveness. Then look at your environment and create a ritual respecting what you see there. Execute the ritual with at least three other people in your community.

"It is imperative that we be aware of our impact on the body of Our Mother Earth wherever we go." Luisah Teish

Chapter 3
Passageways: Commitment and Devotion to Sacred Lands

Dear Readers:

We have named this section "Passageways: Commitment and Devotion To Sacred Lands", to identify our intention. We intend to heal the miseducation, which has led to Conquistador Consciousness. Here we will provide guidelines and recommendations for helping you to change your perspective from that of a tourist to that of a devotee of the land.

In order to help you become a devotee of the land, we have listed a number of principles below. In this section, we also discuss acts of devotion that will help you to fulfill your commitment to the land and the people.

In accordance with the principles outlined in this book, we will provide an online forum for discussion, and require that a class in Holy Grounds Devotional Practices be completed before we finalize registration for any of our passages.

This learning includes an oath to become a caretaker of rivers, land, animals and people. In addition to rituals, you will be given the opportunity to perform actual work such as cleaning the riverbank, attending wildlife preserves and sharing resources with local people.

Fulfillment of these requirements will result in a Certificate of Completion and an invitation to join the Holy Grounds Devotees Ritual Circle.

Guidelines and Recommendations for Sacred Intention

Greetings and Salutations

Greetings and salutations may differ from country to country and from one culture to another within a country. In our classes, we will teach the appropriate greetings and salutations to participate in any and all ceremonies.

Teish's Example:

In keeping with the directives of the elders of Yoruba land and other sacred cultures, we will always begin our passages with a visit to regional temples and/or to receive the blessings and permission of the elders. For example: upon arriving in southwest Nigeria, the honorable practice is a salutation to the Oni of Ile Ife. If one is going to the Oshun shrine in Oshogbo, it is proper protocol to salute the Iyalode, the head Oshun priestess, receive her blessing, then make offerings at the river and bath to receive healings of fertility and prosperity.

Leilani's Example:

If you are meeting an elder in Hawai'i it is the custom to give a lei offering to them and if possible to research the type of flower in the lei to symbolize your gesture. When going to the Big Island of Hawai'i, I must always go to visit Tutu (Grandma) Pele to ask permission to see if the work being done is ok with Her.

Photographing

This section is really important, as we have centuries of tourist taking photos of indigenous people and exploiting them through publishing and misinformation. **Do not assume you can photograph or record people, sacred objects or ceremonies.** On our passages, we will ascertain when and where it is blessed to photograph.

Teish's Example:

There are different rules regarding permission to photograph. In parts of Nigeria, you will find performances and presentations that are provided for people who want to photograph the bright costumes and the artwork of the people. However, there are several sacred ceremonies that must never be photographed even if they are being displayed publicly. Of especial notice is the masquerade Egungun. On occasion dancers arrive wearing the regalia of the ancestors and perform many interesting and stimulating dances and "tricks". At this time, the Egungun may speak prophecy and give directives.

However, they are not to be photographed.

I myself made the mistake of taking several photos of the Egungun from my Baba's compound in Ile Ife. However, before the visit was over a series of events occurred that inspired me to destroy the film I had taken. This is not to be played with.

In general, it is taboo to film or photograph the "Yawo", the initiate who is dressed all in white, and it is absolutely forbidden to photograph the "Odu pot" and several other artifacts of the Women's Secret Societies.

Leilani's Example:

Under no circumstances is it ever appropriate to take pictures of a ceremony without first getting the consent of the group leader. If photographing the ceremony is allowed, then it is assumed by the leader that you are only using this for your personal collection. Photos of ceremony should not be used for public or business purposes when the gift of picture taking has been granted. When you do take pictures, please make sure to make copies available to those you have captured on film, as a gesture of thanks. The same goes for videography as well as audio recordings. Note that ownership should not be something that you are intending when offering your services and this is not an opportunity for professional profiteering or publicity.

Proper Affirmation

You will be informed of the proper ways to show appreciation, approval and affirmation at public events. Do not assume that the western practice of applause is respected everywhere.

Teish's Example:

During my visits to the Maraes of New Zealand, I experienced their greeting rituals. It consisted of being escorted onto the land by a native woman who sang my presence to the village. As they accepted my arrival, I was invited to respond by singing. In the villages of West Africa, one shows approval and kinship by calling out the word Ase, loudly and repeatedly. This is very different from entering the temples of Japan or Southeast Asia where one bows in silence.

Leilani's Example:

In Hawaii, during a Hula performance it is customary to shout and interact with the dancer as a participant. When a dance is finished the audience often shouts 'hana hou' which means, please do this again, sing another song and dance more for us. While performing at a closing ceremony at

Michigan Women's Music Festival, the officiating Priestess Ruth Barrett, would direct the audience to simply wave fingers and hands in the air, at the end of the performance and to refrain from applause. This was done to move the mindset of the audience from performance mode to ritual and sacred space mode.

The Sacred Zone

Our trips to sacred lands will be drug, alcohol, and tobacco free, except in cases where these substances are a part of the offering. No recreational drugs, alcohol, or tobacco will ever be allowed.

Teish's Example:

Upon visiting shrines in Nigeria, it is appropriate to offer bottles of rum, gin, or schnapps to the keepers of the shrine. It is only appropriate to have a drink if offered by the elder. Most often, a drink is offered as part of a ceremony and not as a social act. In the traditions coming out of Cuba and other Caribbean Islands, it is customary to light and smoke a cigar. After a while, the shaman will go into trance and the cigar smoke is used to clean the aura of participants and is sometimes used to show the person's imperviousness to fire by running the lit cigar along their bare skin without consequence.

This issue is of especial importance to me because I had too many sacred site tours filled with participants who were simply looking for a cheap way to get away from home and display drunken behavior. It was this disrespectful behavior that caused me to stop offering trips.

Leilani's Example:

Do not see a sacred sites pilgrimage as a vacation but rather as a prayer space. This is a 'party free' zone. Fun will be had but it will be under the influence of community and prayer rather than substance abuse. If you cannot put down your beer or wine for the duration of a sacred pilgrimage, then perhaps it is time to explore issues around addiction. Allow yourself to attain altered states of consciousness by traveling through the veil between the worlds rather than through substances. In very specific and tightly guided containers, medicine people have used sacred plants and herbs. However, it is always highly recommended that you learn to journey to the spirit world through your own devotion and connection to spirit through ceremony and prayer.

Respecting Natural Resources

Do not pick native plants, stones, and shells, without proper permission. We will clarify right actions with the local elders.

Teish's Example:

In the early days of my priesthood training, I went with an elder of mine to pick wild herbs for an important ritual. He identified the plant to be harvested and I began attempting to cut the plant. Each time I reached for the plant, known as Spanish Bayonet Palm, one of the sharp pointed leaves would prick me and make a little mark on my skin. After several tries, the elder came over to me and asked if I had properly asked the plant for its permission to harvest it. When I replied that I had not, he said "Well, no wonder it is defending itself." He then taught me the appropriate prayers and songs, told me never to devastate the Mother plant, and gave me much more information about the temperament and the use of the plant. On our journeys we will remember that all of nature is alive and due our respect, and we will consult with local elders who can teach us the respectful ways to approach these natural resources.

Leilani's Example:

Hawaiians also believe it is a necessity to ask the permission of plants that are to be used for medicinal, food and ceremonial purposes. While searching for plants, herbs and flowers, a plant will show that it is giving permission and offering itself a number of ways including waving in the wind or shaking. Mindfulness and observation are needed in order to hear the soft whispers of our plant Ohana/family. In addition, it is never appropriate to take rocks or stones from Hawai'i. There are countless stories of tourists who are bombarded with bad luck after breaking this protocol. Rocks and stones are known to be sent back to the Islands hoping to reverse the bad luck bestowed upon them.

The Marketplace

Tourism puts such a great emphasis on bringing people to the marketplace. Most often, this is done so that visitors can purchase artifacts cheaply for their personal use. However, there has been much exploitation of indigenous people by merchants who purchase with arrogance and sell at a higher price in another location.

It is important to be supportive of local artisans and craftspeople but that support should come in the form of respect as well as money. By exhibiting respect and establishing a relationship with the market people, we will assure an invitation to authentic events and avoid those trinkets that are set up for tourists.

Teish's Example:

While traveling through Benin, for ritual purposes, I checked into a hotel (the equivalent of a Howard Johnson's) and was mistaken for a tourist by a local man. This man approached me the way an American pimp would and had to be put in his place. When I told him that I was a priestess of Oshun, he excused himself and apologized for mistaking me for a tourist. On another occasion, a local man attempted to sell me a baby gazelle as bush meat. The only way to avoid such confrontations is to be guided and directed by the respected elders of the villages.

Leilani's Example:

Supporting local vendors and artisans is always a wonderful way to give back to the land you are visiting. I try to support Native Hawaiian artists when traveling home. It is important to find information on the artists you are patronizing, as unfortunately there are those who are making big bucks off the images of native peoples but are not from that tradition. I know of a famous photographer in Hawaii who does beautiful black and white imagery of Hula dancers in sacred motion and prayer. This particular photographer claimed that the positions of the dancers were his property and could not be used by other artist, even the indigenous ones. Of course, we know that Hula cannot be owned or copyrighted. It rests in the care of the Kumu Hula masters who teach our sacred dance.

Environmental Impact

It is imperative that we be aware of our impact on the body of Our Mother Earth wherever we go. We will always strive to do no harm, clean up after ourselves, and to participate in the efforts of local people to steward the land. Those considering our passages must know that Earth Stewardship is an integral part of our reasons for any journey we undertake.

Teish's Example:

I have traveled around the globe at least twice in my lifetime. In every place, whether I am in Africa, South America, Australia, or Southeast Asia, it only takes a few days before the local people show me a gaping hole in the Earth, polluted waterways, or communities in dire poverty, with an explanation of the role my country and government have played in their demise. As a child of nature and a citizen of the world, I explain that I am one of the people who recognize our kinship and have dedicated my life to healing this wound. That statement must always be followed by an action that demonstrates sincerity and helps to improve the conditions of the world. Sometimes it is as simple as picking up trash on the seashore, or visiting sick children with a story telling session. In my experience, all such acts, sincerely offered, are received with love, respect, and kinship.

Leilani's Example:

The fresh sweet water is the most precious and sacred resource on Hawaii. Islands surrounded by salt water for 1000's of miles are dependent on the rainwaters that are bestowed upon the land. The word wai is the word for water and the term wai wai means abundance and wealth. Water is wealth and prosperity. The abuse of water rights on almost all of the islands is a huge political issue. It is not uncommon to see what were once the lush fertile valleys of taro plants, dried up as tunnels divert sweet water to hotels, golf courses, and tourist areas. This is done without any consideration for the original native peoples of the land or how this might affect generations of farming and aquaculture. Many people have been left in areas that look like tropical deserts. Know that when you visit the islands and take a sip of the sweet water in your glass, shower in your hotel room, or see the green of your golf course, there is a piece of land in Hawaii that is suffering as are Her people.

Original Tapa Cloth

Exercise 3: Finding Holy Ground

There are many places on the Earth that are well known and regarded as Holy: The Pyramids of Egypt, the Mountains of Peru, the Waterfalls of Brazil, and the Migration routes of South Africa just to name a few.

In this exercise, we would like to expand your notion of Holy Ground by doing the following:

Find a spot in your city or town, determine and name its holiness. Is it a place where tragedies (such as bicycle accidents or gang violence have occurred) or a place of great beauty and joy? What can you do to cause it to become recognized and treated as holy?

For example: Placing flowers where the accident occurred or planting trees in honor of those killed in gang violence on that spot.

Think about the region of the country you live in (Pacific Northwest, South East, North East etc). Can you uncover some people's history that identifies Holy Ground?

Now think of the country you live in (United States, Mexico, or China). Where would you like to establish Holy Ground?

And when you think or dream of international travel to a sacred site where do you most want to go?

Make a list of these places, write a few paragraphs exploring your interests, and determine what actions you can take to establish Holy Ground.

<u>Closing Prayer: On Holy Ground</u>

An Oath to Mother Earth and Her Children

I_____child of Mother Earth and
Father Sky do hereby;

Make a commitment to devote myself to the sacredness of the
lands upon where I stand, walk, sleep, or pass.

I vow to do no harm and yet even to make each place whereon
I walk better for my having been there.

I agree to defend the people, the animals and the spirits of
every land against exploitation, to respect them and to hold
them as precious and sacred.

I commit to overcoming the beliefs, and behaviors that may
have separated me from nature and spirit in the past. And
I commit to educating myself on the ecology, mythology and
traditions of many lands to nurture an awareness of my place
in relationship to the spirits and the people of those lands.

I ask the Elders, the Ancestors, and the Spirits of the lands
to guide me in Right Conduct as I fulfill my commitment and
devotion to Holy Grounds.

<u>Signed:</u> _____

<u>Date:</u> _____

Earth Lovers Endorsements, Ashe-Aloha

We give praise and thanks to the following people who have written review comments for us and whose organizations, contact, and work are listed below:

"Come home. To our gorgeous planet. Your tour guides: two of the most powerful, embodied priestesses of our time. This book is rich with stories, visions, and sacred practices, bringing time-honored indigenous Earth-based wisdom and ritual into the 21st century. The healing, joyful, and transformative power of this text is accessible to all, at once deeply poetic and completely practical. A must-read for those who want to participate in our planetary transformation."

Cassandra Vieten, PhD
Director of Research
Institute of Noetic Sciences
cvieten@noetic.org

"The book moves between a call for a shift in consciousness, as illustrated so beautifully by your stories and experiences, and several sets of instructions for people to follow in order to shift their own consciousness. I think it is an urgently-needed and timely discussion of these issues, and it is so beautifully written. Thank you again for the privilege of being one of your readers."

Caitlin Sislin
Women's Earth Alliance
Caitlin@womensearthalliance.org
The David Brower Center
2150 Allston Way, Suite 460 Berkeley, CA 94704
info@womensearthalliance.org
510-859-9110
Women's Earth Alliance is an Earth Island Institute Organization
510-541-0271

"On Holy Ground: Commitment and Devotion to Sacred Lands is a practical and inspirational resource guide in how we can all reconnect and care for the sacred lands. The rituals and practices provide ways that we can engage, equip and empower each other to care for our essential home, Mother Earth."

Angeles Arrien Ph.D.
Cultural anthropologist
Author of The Four Fold Way
www.angelesarrien.com

Other Supporters

Jyoti Spiritual Director
Carol Hart Media director
Ann Rosencranz, Program
info@grandmotherscouncil.com
www.grandmotherscouncil.com
www.sacredstudies.org
www.forthenext7generations.com

Wangari Maathai
Lantern Books
128 Second Place
Garden Suite
Brooklyn, New York 11231

The Giveaway
Ojai Foundation
P.O. Box 5037
Ojai, CA 93023

Paloma Pavel-Earth House
Palomapavel@yahoo.com
510-469-7777

Breakthrough Communities
5275 Miles Avenue
Oakland, CA 94618
p: 510-652-2425
f: 510-595-7295
Connect@EarthHouseCenter.org
www.breakthroughcommunities.info

Mary Gonzales
Gamaliel
203 North Wabash Avenue, Suite 808
Chicago, Illinois 60601
510-290-6955
Toll Free: 888-812-5831
Local: 312-357-2639
Fax: 312-357-6735
E-mail: info@gamaliel.org
Email: gamaliel-ca@sbcglobal.net

Our contact information

Luisah Teish
5111 Telegraph Ave.
Private Mail Box #305
Oakland, CA 94609
DahomeyRoyal@gmail.com
www.luisahteish.com

Leilani Birely
3527 Mt. Diablo Blvd. #353
Lafayette, CA 94549
Leilani@DaughtersoftheGoddess.com
www.DaughtersoftheGoddess.com

CPSIA information can be obtained
at www.ICGtesting.com
Printed in the USA
FSHW011146070320
67786FS